A STORY OF FAMILY RESTORATION

Arthur Thompson

Publisher: Upway Books
Authors: Arthur Thompson
Title: A STORY OF FAMILY RESTORATION
ISBN: 978-1-917916-59-2
Cover Designed on Canva: www.canva.com

contact@upwaybooks.com
www.upwaybooks.com

Contents

Introduction

Family is the foundation of who we are. It shapes our beliefs, our values, and often our sense of identity. But what happens when that foundation is cracked—through trauma, loss, or disconnection?

This book, A Story of Family Restoration, is my journey toward rebuilding, healing, and reconnecting with the people and principles that make us whole. It is also an invitation for you to explore how restorative practices can transform families, communities, and even lives.

I was raised by my grandparents—two wise and loving individuals who carried the strength and resilience of generations before me. They taught me what it meant to be grounded in love, discipline, and tradition, even as they navigated their own struggles. Growing up as a Black male in a world that often stereotypes and misunderstands us, I leaned heavily on the lessons my grandparents instilled: the value of respect, the power of accountability, and the necessity of compassion.

But even with their guidance, there were moments when our family faced fractures—moments of silence, misunderstanding, and pain that seemed too heavy to repair. It was through those moments that I discovered a restorative practice framework—not just for resolving conflict, but for rebuilding relationships, creating safe spaces, and fostering connection.

A Message to You

This book is not just about my story—it's about yours. Whether you're navigating family struggles, seeking to mend broken relationships, or simply searching for a deeper connection with the people you love, I hope this book offers tools, inspiration, and hope.

Restoration is possible, and it begins with the belief that every family—no matter how broken—can find its way back to wholeness. As you read, I encourage you to reflect on the relationships in your life: father, mother, sisters, and brothers. Who do you need to restore with? What conversations have you avoided? What wounds still need healing?

Together, we'll explore how restorative practices can provide a roadmap for reconciliation—not just in our families, but in our communities and beyond. There is work to be done—first within ourselves, and then with those around us.

On a personal level, healing starts with acknowledgment. It means recognizing the pain or trauma you carry and allowing yourself to feel it without guilt or shame. Whether it's physical healing after an injury or emotional healing after loss or hardship, the steps are similar.

For Black communities around the globe, healing often involves addressing centuries of systemic injustice, intergenerational trauma, and the ongoing fight for equity. At the same time, it's about celebrating resilience, culture, and shared joy.

Healing is also about creating a better future for the next generation. It's the work of breaking cycles of pain and trauma through education, empowerment, and joy.

Chapter 1: The Dysfunction

For generations, grandparents have played a pivotal role in raising children when parents are unable to. This dynamic is especially common in Black communities, often because of systemic challenges such as incarceration, substance abuse, economic hardship, or untimely death—events that disrupt the traditional family structure.

Grandparents bring wisdom, love, and a sense of stability—but their role is not without difficulty, both for them and for the children they raise. In my case, the issue was divorce. My parents separated when I was three, and my sister was eleven months older than me. After the divorce, we went to live with our grandparents. My grandmother was the dominant figure in our family, while my mother battled health issues.

Your grandparents may love you deeply, but there's often a gap in understanding your world. They may struggle to fully grasp the pressures of growing up as a young Black man today—whether that means confronting systemic racism, navigating school challenges, or dealing with social dynamics like peer pressure or gang influence.

Every family has its own story, its own rhythm, its own way of being. For me, that rhythm was often fractured, uneven, and filled with silence. My grandparents were the foundation of our home—two strong-willed individuals who carried the weight of generations past and the hope for generations to come. They had left the small, tight-knit communities of the South in search of opportunity in the city—a migration story familiar to many Black families of their time. But with that move came disconnection, new challenges, and unspoken truths that shaped the dynamics of our household in ways I didn't fully understand until much later.

A House of Silence

In our family, we didn't talk about the hard things. In fact, we didn't talk much at all. Communication was one-sided. As children, my sister and I were expected to listen, obey, and stay in our place. Adults were the authority, and any questioning of that authority was met with swift correction.

Questions like *"Why?"* or *"What's going on?"* simply weren't part of the vocabulary in our home. There were family secrets—some I wouldn't uncover until years later—that lingered in the air like invisible walls between us. We all lived under the same roof, but emotionally, we were distant.

My grandparents worked hard to provide for us, but their focus on survival left little room for nurturing deeper connections. My mother lived with us too, but she wasn't active in raising my sister or me. She was there physically, but not emotionally, and not involved in shaping who we were becoming.

Looking back, I see the dysfunction for what it was: a family trying to hold itself together under the weight of unspoken pain, generational trauma, and cultural expectations. But as a child, I didn't have the words for what I was experiencing. I only knew that something felt missing.

For older generations—especially those who lived through segregation, war, or systemic oppression—trauma was often internalized as *"just the way things are."* Revisiting it felt dangerous, even unbearable, so it was easier to stay silent.

The Legacy of the South

My grandparents, like so many Black families of their generation, carried the unspoken rules of the South into our home. They had grown up in an era where survival often depended on staying quiet, staying small, and not drawing attention. Those lessons—shaped by systemic racism and economic hardship—defined how they parented.

They believed in discipline, structure, and respect for authority. These values had served them well in a world where stepping out of line could have dire consequences. But those same lessons often left little room for vulnerability, openness, or emotional honesty. You didn't challenge authority. You didn't air dirty laundry. And you certainly didn't talk about the past.

For them, silence was a survival tactic. For us, their grandchildren, it became a barrier. Sometimes silence grows from shame—shame tied to past mistakes, family secrets, or abuse. Speaking up can feel like exposing too much or breaking a sacred family code.

During slavery, enslaved African families were intentionally torn apart—parents separated from children, husbands from wives, communities dismantled. Those forced separations left deep scars that still shape how Black families connect and communicate today. Many enslaved individuals had to suppress emotion just to survive. The need to *"be strong"* and avoid vulnerability became ingrained, creating cycles of emotional silence.

Understanding what we inherit—and how we inherit it—is essential if we hope to make changes, to overcome what we experienced growing up, and to stop transferring that pain to future generations.

The Emotional Distance

I loved my grandparents deeply, and I know they loved me in the ways they knew how. But love in our household was often expressed through action—through providing, through discipline, through making sure we had what we needed. Emotional connection, however, was harder to come by.

It wasn't that they didn't care. It was that they had been taught that love was shown through sacrifice, not words. They were products of their time, their culture, and their circumstances. But for a child trying to make sense of the world, the lack of emotional closeness left a void. I often felt like I was navigating life alone, even in a house full of people.

Action-based love is powerful, but it can feel different for each family member. There's something sacred about a parent cooking your favorite meal, a sibling helping you with homework, or a grandfather slipping you a few dollars *"just because."* These actions hold weight and communicate care in deeply meaningful ways.

Action-based love instills values of hard work, responsibility, and care for others. It creates stability and safety. Yet it also brings challenges. Without verbal or emotional affirmation, family members may sometimes feel unseen—even when deeply loved. A child might wonder, *"Do they love me?"* because love was not spoken, even though it was shown.

In such households, emotions often remain unspoken. Members might bottle things up or avoid conflict, creating distance. And while actions communicate care, they can't always replace the need for affection, encouragement, or a simple *"I'm proud of you."*

The Weight of Secrets

The silence in our home didn't just extend to daily communication—it also covered the things that were too painful or shameful to discuss. There were family secrets that everyone seemed to know but no one dared to acknowledge.

These secrets created an invisible tension, a sense that something was always just beneath the surface that no one wanted to disturb. I've come to realize that these secrets weren't unique to my family. Many families, especially Black families carrying the legacies of trauma and systemic oppression, shoulder similar burdens.

But as a child, I didn't understand why certain topics were off-limits, why certain questions went unanswered, or why certain truths were hidden in plain sight.

Living in Dysfunction

Growing up in a dysfunctional family isn't always obvious when you're in the middle of it—it just feels normal. You don't realize that the lack of communication, the emotional distance, or the unspoken rules are shaping how you see the world and yourself.

For me, dysfunction looked like a house where emotions were suppressed, where love was shown but rarely spoken, and where each person carried their own struggles in silence. It looked like a mother who was present but absent, grandparents who gave everything they had but couldn't give what they hadn't received themselves, and a family that didn't know how to bridge the gaps between us.

Growing Up in the Inner City

Growing up as a Black male in the inner city was a journey filled with challenges, lessons, and a constant need to adapt. As a young boy, I didn't yet understand the intricacies of the world around me. I was simply living—trying to make sense of my environment and learning how to navigate a life that was often unpredictable.

The streets had their own set of rules, and I had to learn how to maneuver through distractions, temptations, and hardships. Some lessons came the hard way—through costly mistakes—while others came through moments of clarity and resilience.

The Streets Were a Classroom

In the inner city, the streets became a classroom, though not in the traditional sense. I learned survival skills from watching and listening— how to read people, how to avoid trouble, and sometimes, how to blend in with the crowd. These weren't lessons taught by a teacher or found in a textbook. They were learned through lived experience—both good and bad.

Distractions were everywhere: the temptations of fast money, the allure of fitting in with the wrong crowd, and the constant pull to escape the reality of my circumstances. The streets didn't offer a safety net. One wrong move, one bad decision, could have lasting consequences.

And while I wanted to succeed, I lacked the tools, guidance, and structure to stay focused. Looking back, I realize I was navigating a maze without a map. I didn't yet have the skills to manage conflict, process my emotions, or make decisions that would set me on a better path. Instead, I figured things out as I went—often paying the price for my lack of preparation.

High School: A Missed Opportunity

High school should have been a time of growth, discovery, and preparation for the future. For me, it became something entirely different. It was more of a hangout spot than a place of learning. I went to class, but my mind wasn't there. I was physically present but mentally absent.

Low grades became the norm, and so did my absences. I didn't see the value in school, and no one had instilled in me the importance of education as a way out—or a way up. Without direction or motivation, I floated through those years, living day to day without any sense of purpose or plan for the future.

It wasn't just about academics. High school was a reflection of the larger world I was trying to navigate. There were conflicts—some small, others significant—but I didn't know how to handle them. My instinct was either to avoid them altogether or to react emotionally, which often made things worse. I had no conflict management skills, no tools to de-escalate tension, and no idea how to resolve issues constructively.

The Cost of Poor Decisions

Some of the decisions I made during this time were costly— emotionally, financially, and socially. I lost opportunities, damaged relationships, and created setbacks that took years to recover from.

At the time, I didn't fully understand the weight of my choices. I was just trying to survive, to make it through each day, without realizing how my actions would shape my future. But life has a way of teaching us, even when we're unwilling students. Every mistake, every misstep carried a lesson.

Some of those lessons were painful, but they were necessary. They forced me to confront myself, to recognize where I was falling short, and to start thinking about the kind of life I wanted to build.

Learning Through Experience

Much of my childhood and teenage years were shaped by dysfunction and a lack of guidance, but they also gave me something valuable: resilience. I learned how to adapt, how to keep moving forward even when the odds were stacked against me.

I didn't have conflict management skills back then, but I began to develop a sense of awareness—of what worked and what didn't, of the kind of person I didn't want to become.

The lessons from those years weren't easy, but they laid the foundation for growth that would come later. They taught me that failure isn't final, that mistakes don't define you, and that even in chaos, there are opportunities to learn and grow.

Chapter 2: The Turning Point

I was headed nowhere fast. My life felt like a cycle of bad decisions, missed opportunities, and a lack of direction. I didn't have a plan, a purpose, or even the tools to figure out what I wanted. Deep down, I knew I needed something to turn my life around. I couldn't keep going the way I was.

I had only one relationship that truly mattered, and many surface-level acquaintances. I realized I needed something beyond myself— something to measure and guide my life by.

Growing up, I went to Sunday School. My grandfather used to drop me off, and I attended all the church activities—VBS, Boy Scouts, and more. Those early experiences planted seeds that, at my lowest point, began to surface and became a source of strength.

Now, as a father with a family of my own, I needed stability—not just for me, but for them. At my lowest point, I remembered a simple truth: *"Jesus loves me."* That's when I started attending church again.

At first, I didn't know what to expect. I just knew I needed something different—not another place to go, not another routine to fill time, but something deeper. It was there, in that space of worship and reflection, that I began to feel something shift inside me. I didn't know it then, but I was being drawn toward something greater than myself.

Giving My Life to the Lord

The day I gave my life to the Lord was the day everything began to change. It wasn't an instant transformation—life doesn't work that way—but it was the start of a new chapter.

For the first time, I felt hope—a belief that my life could be different. Faith gave me something I had been missing for so long: purpose. It gave me a reason to wake up in the morning, to try harder, and to believe that I was capable of more.

It also gave me a community—a group of people who supported me, encouraged me, and held me accountable.

A New Passion and Focus

With faith as my foundation, my focus became clearer. I started to see the bigger picture of my life—the potential I had and the steps I needed to take to get there.

Discipline, something I had always struggled with, began to take root. I learned that discipline wasn't about forcing myself to do things I didn't want to do—it was about aligning my actions with my goals and values. It was about making choices that reflected the person I wanted to become, not the person I had been.

As one writer put it, *"Self-discipline is the bridge between goals defined and goals accomplished."*

Faith taught me to trust—not just in God, but in myself and in others. For so long, I had carried the weight of my struggles alone, believing I couldn't rely on anyone else. But through faith, I discovered the power of community—of leaning on others for support and realizing I didn't have to do it all on my own.

Building Discipline Through Faith

Discipline became a cornerstone of my new life. It wasn't easy at first. I had to unlearn old habits and replace them with new ones. I had to hold myself accountable in ways I never had before.

But with each small step, I began to see progress. Faith gave me the strength to stay consistent, even when it was hard. It reminded me that discipline wasn't just about achieving goals—it was about becoming the person God called me to be.

As one guide on self-discipline explains, *"Consistency in your actions and behavior is what leads to long-term success."*

I started small—showing up on time, completing tasks, staying committed to responsibilities. Over time, those small wins added up, and I began to see the power of discipline in action.

Trusting the Process

One of the hardest lessons I had to learn was to trust the process. Change doesn't happen overnight, and there were moments when I wanted to give up. But faith reminded me that growth takes time, and every step forward—no matter how small—was progress.

I also had to learn to trust others. For years, I built walls around myself, believing vulnerability was weakness. But faith taught me that trust is strength. It allows you to build deeper relationships, learn from others, and grow in ways you never could alone.

Steps to Transformation

1. Breaking Down the Walls of Denial

The first step in breaking the cycle of dysfunction is acknowledging its existence. Denial is a powerful barrier that keeps families trapped in harmful patterns. By honestly acknowledging dysfunction, individuals open the door to self-awareness and begin the journey toward transformation. It takes courage to confront painful realities, but it's a necessary catalyst for change.

2. Unearthing the Root Causes

To truly address dysfunction, we must uncover its roots. Urban families often face external challenges—poverty, violence, limited resources—that contribute to unhealthy dynamics. Historical trauma and intergenerational struggles also play a role. By understanding these causes, families gain insight into their behaviors and begin breaking the chains that bind them.

3. Cultivating Healthy Communication

Communication is the lifeblood of any relationship, and its importance is magnified in urban families. Dysfunction thrives in silence and miscommunication. Proactive, open communication fosters empathy, understanding, and problem-solving. By actively listening, expressing feelings honestly, and seeking compromise, family members can rebuild trust and connection.

4. Embracing Emotional Resilience

Urban families often face high levels of stress and trauma. Building emotional resilience helps navigate these challenges without succumbing to despair. Resilience grows through support networks, therapy, self-care, and positive coping mechanisms. It enables individuals to endure hardship while steering their lives toward hope and stability.

5. Rewriting the Narrative

Dysfunctional patterns often pass from generation to generation as learned behavior. To break this cycle, families must rewrite their narrative—choosing stories of triumph over trauma. This means challenging limiting beliefs, fostering growth mindsets, and setting higher expectations. Empowering future generations with education,

opportunity, and positive values paves the way for a new legacy—
one rooted in strength and fulfillment.

6. Building a Supportive Network

Breaking free from dysfunction requires support. Community
organizations, support groups, and local resources can provide safe
spaces to share experiences and access guidance. Connecting with
others who've walked similar paths reminds families they are not
alone in their journey toward healing.

7. Establishing Boundaries

Dysfunction often thrives where boundaries are weak or non-
existent. Establishing clear boundaries fosters healthy relationships
and respect. This includes defining personal space, setting behavioral
limits, and enforcing consequences. Healthy boundaries require
honesty, communication, and mutual respect.

8. Seeking Professional Help

Therapists, counselors, and social workers can be invaluable allies in
breaking cycles of dysfunction. Professional guidance helps families
process trauma, resolve conflict, and develop new coping strategies.
Seeking help is not a sign of weakness—it's a courageous step
toward change.

9. Nurturing Self-Esteem and Self-Worth

Dysfunction erodes confidence and self-belief. Rebuilding self-worth involves practicing positive self-talk, celebrating progress, and focusing on growth. When individuals begin to see themselves as capable and deserving, they open the door to transformation.

10. Emphasizing Education and Lifelong Learning

Education is one of the most powerful tools for breaking cycles of dysfunction. Encouraging children to value learning, supporting academic success, and fostering curiosity create opportunities that extend far beyond the classroom.

11. Celebrating Small Victories

Every step toward healing deserves recognition. Whether it's overcoming a personal obstacle or improving communication, celebrating progress reinforces hope and builds momentum for continued growth.

12. The Power of Perseverance

Breaking free from dysfunction is a long journey filled with setbacks and breakthroughs. Perseverance is the key. Families must remind themselves that change takes time—but with commitment and resilience, transformation is not only possible, it's inevitable.

Chapter 3: The Restorative Practices Journey

A Black male trying to live restoratively in the late 1960s and early 1970s was fighting both outer wars—racism and poverty—and inner wars—family silence and emotional denial. He was trying to break generational cycles at a time when "healing" wasn't even a word most families used yet.

Family Dysfunction for a Black Male (Late 1960s–Early 1970s)

During this era, a Black male striving to live restoratively would be navigating forms of family dysfunction that looked like this:

Generational Trauma:

Many Black families were still carrying deep wounds from segregation, Jim Crow laws, and migration from the South. Trauma wasn't openly discussed—it was inherited and often normalized. Restoration meant trying to heal while everyone else was saying, *"Just survive."*

Silence Around Emotions:

Expressing vulnerability, sadness, or hurt wasn't encouraged—especially for Black men. "Man up." "Don't cry." These were survival tactics passed down because the outside world was already hostile.

Financial Hardship and Instability:

Many families faced poverty, underemployment, housing discrimination (redlining), and lack of access to quality education. Dysfunction often looked like constant financial stress that led to arguments, absentee parents working multiple jobs, or untreated mental health issues.

Substance Abuse and Escapism:

The late '60s and '70s saw a rise in drug use—particularly heroin in urban Black communities—stemming from systemic neglect and despair. Some family members coped by disappearing into addiction.

Denial and Image Maintenance:

Outward respectability—keeping up appearances at church or in the neighborhood—often mattered more than confronting the real, messy problems inside the home. Living restoratively meant wanting to tell the truth when others preferred to pretend.

Generational Gaps:

Civil Rights activism was surging, yet older family members who had lived through harsher racism often clashed with younger, more militant ones (think traditional respectability versus the Black Panther movement). A young man seeking peace and restoration might feel caught between two generations of pain and expectation.

Religious Pressure:

Many Black families were deeply rooted in the church, but religion was sometimes used to silence rather than heal—"pray it away" instead of addressing real emotional wounds. Living restoratively meant pushing for authentic healing beyond religious appearances.

The Call to Serve

After my own transformation, I knew I couldn't keep the lessons I'd learned to myself. My life had been turned around, and I felt a deep calling to live with discipline and purpose—not just for my own benefit, but to serve others.

That's what community truly is: pouring into others as others have poured into you.

With this renewed sense of purpose, I pursued ministry. I received my license to preach and embraced the opportunity to share the message of hope and restoration that had changed my life. But I soon realized that ministry wasn't confined to the walls of a church building—it was bigger than that. Ministry could happen anywhere, and I was being called to take that message beyond the pulpit.

The Challenge to Serve Beyond the Church

One of the most pivotal moments in my journey came when a former pastor challenged me to think beyond traditional ministry. He told me, *"If you're called to preach, then go find somewhere to preach and serve."*

Those words stayed with me. They pushed me out of my comfort zone and into new spaces—places where the message of restoration was needed most. That challenge led me somewhere I never expected: a jail in Washington, D.C.

At first, I didn't know what to expect. I had never imagined myself preaching in a jail, but I knew I was being called there. In that environment, I was introduced to Prison Fellowship, an organization dedicated to bringing hope and transformation to incarcerated individuals.

Ministry in Jail

Serving in jail was unlike anything I had ever experienced. It was raw, real, and humbling. The men I met weren't just inmates—they were fathers, sons, brothers, and men with stories of pain, brokenness, and redemption.

Many of them had grown up in environments like mine, facing the same struggles and distractions. I quickly realized that ministry in jail wasn't about preaching *at* people—it was about listening, connecting, and meeting them where they were. It was about showing them that their past didn't have to define their future, and that restoration was possible no matter how far they had fallen.

Through Prison Fellowship, I learned to approach ministry with empathy and humility. I saw firsthand the power of faith to transform lives, even in the hardest circumstances. And I began to understand that my journey—my struggles, my mistakes, my redemption—wasn't just for me. It was meant to be shared, to inspire others, and to show them that change is possible.

Finding Purpose in Service

Purpose is one of the most powerful forces in life. It gives direction, meaning, and a reason to wake up each day with intention. I found my purpose not in seeking personal gain or recognition, but in serving others.

It was through service that I discovered who I was meant to be—and how I could make a meaningful impact on the world.

The Power of Service

Service has a way of shifting your focus from yourself to the needs of others. It challenges you to step outside your comfort zone and see the world through a different lens. As one source says, *"In life, we achieve purpose by serving others. The need for significance is fundamental to our existence, and we find it when we look beyond ourselves."*

When I began serving in ministry—especially in the jail setting—I realized that service wasn't just about helping others; it was about transformation. It transformed their lives, but it also transformed mine. It taught me humility, compassion, and the importance of living for something greater than myself.

Purpose Beyond the Self

True purpose lies beyond self. It's not about what you achieve for yourself, but what you contribute to others. As one source puts it, *"To create a sustainable impact that goes beyond quarterly statements, leaders need to embrace a purpose beyond themselves."*

For me, this meant using my experiences—the struggles and the triumphs—to inspire and uplift others. It meant recognizing that my journey wasn't just about me. It was about the people I could reach, the lives I could touch, and the communities I could help restore.

Serving in Ministry

When I began serving in jail, I witnessed firsthand the power of service to bring hope and healing. Many of the men I met were searching for purpose, longing to move beyond their mistakes and build better futures.

Through Prison Fellowship, I was able to show them that purpose is possible, even in the most challenging circumstances. I learned that ministry isn't about having all the answers or fixing every problem. It's about showing up, being present, listening deeply, and offering hope.

Serving in jail deepened my understanding of what it means to live a purposeful life. It's not about recognition or accolades. It's about being willing to go where you're needed, even if it's uncomfortable or unexpected. It's about using your experiences—both the good and the bad—to make a difference in the lives of others.

For me, ministry became more than a calling—it became a way of life. It taught me that purpose isn't something you *find*; it's something you *create* through service, discipline, and trust in God's plan.

A Life of Purpose

Finding purpose in service has been one of the most rewarding aspects of my life. It has given me a fulfillment no material success could ever provide. It has reminded me that we are all connected—and that our greatest impact comes not from what we take, but from what we give.

As one source beautifully puts it, *"Your service can be your purpose."*

Healing the Self: Rebuilding from Within

Living on purpose requires healing the wounds that dysfunction creates. Healing doesn't erase the past—it allows you to reclaim your power.

Invest in Mental and Emotional Wellness

- Seek therapy if available, particularly culturally affirming therapy. Initiatives like *The Loveland Foundation* or *Black Men Heal* provide mental health resources for people of color.

- Engage in mindfulness practices—journaling, prayer, meditation, or art therapy—to process emotions and find peace.

Lean Into Community Healing

- Build relationships with mentors, elders, or peers who have walked similar paths.

- Participate in local organizations focused on empowerment, such as youth groups or cultural centers.

Healing is both personal and communal. When we do the work within, we strengthen the fabric of the communities around us.

Chapter 4: The Transformation

Moving from self and dysfunction to a life of purpose in the inner city is a transformative journey—one not for the faint of heart. It demands something deeper than survival. It calls for self-awareness, healing, empowerment, and action.

But where does that journey begin?

For a long time, I thought dysfunction was just who I was.

It was the loud arguments in the next room.

It was the missed promises, the absent hugs, the dreams I learned not to speak out loud.

It was the invisible weight I carried through every street corner, every classroom, every job interview.

At first, I didn't even have words for it. I just knew something inside me was tired of pretending everything was fine.

The first step was seeing myself clearly.

Not the mask I wore to survive.

Not the role my family needed me to play.

But the real me—the boy underneath the bruises and bravado who still believed he was worth fighting for.

Self-awareness is both brutal and beautiful. It forces you to face not only what was done to you, but also the ways you learned to hurt yourself. It shines a light into the corners you've been avoiding your whole life.

But in that light, you find your power.

Healing

Healing came next.
Not the kind of healing that happens in one church service or after one good cry. Real healing—the slow, frustrating, sometimes lonely process of forgiving, grieving, and rebuilding.

It meant letting go of needing apologies that would never come. It meant setting boundaries with people who taught me I had no right to set any.

It meant teaching myself a new way to love—one not based on fear or performance.

Empowerment

Then came empowerment—the realization that I didn't have to be a product of my past. That I could be a pattern-breaker, a chain-cutter, a builder of new legacies.

Empowerment wasn't about being perfect. It was about making a decision:

"I refuse to pass down what nearly destroyed me."

Action

And finally, action.

Because purpose without action is just a dream deferred.

Living in the inner city taught me that healing wasn't just personal—it had to be communal. My success wasn't mine to keep; it was mine to share, to pour back into the streets that raised me—the neighborhoods that often broke me but still called me *son*.

The journey from dysfunction to purpose is messy. It's humbling. But it's the most powerful revolution a Black man can lead—not against the world outside, but against the brokenness within.

This book is my offering to anyone standing at that crossroads, wondering if it's possible to choose a different way.

It is.

And it begins with seeing yourself not as broken beyond repair, but as powerful beyond measure.

Inner-city communities often face systemic challenges—poverty, lack of resources, crime, and limited access to education. Yet they are also rich in culture, resilience, and potential. Below, I'll explore how personal growth connects with community upliftment.

Step 1: Recognize the Cycles

To move from dysfunction to purpose, the first step is recognizing the cycles—whether they stem from internal struggles (trauma, self-doubt, lack of vision) or external forces (environmental hardships, systemic oppression).

- **Ask Reflective Questions:** Who am I outside of my circumstances? What patterns in my life are holding me back? What legacy do I want to leave behind?

- **Name the Pain:** Many inner-city environments are shaped by generational trauma and societal neglect. Acknowledging personal pain and its connection to systemic issues can be freeing. This includes facing fears of failure or recognizing coping mechanisms like anger or avoidance.

Step 2: Discover Purpose

Purpose is rooted in understanding your unique skills, passions, and values—and recognizing how they align with serving something greater than yourself. In the context of the inner city, this often means contributing to the upliftment of your community.

- **Discover Your "Why":**
  - What does your life mean? Is it mentoring others, creating art, advocating for justice, or building generational wealth?
  - What challenges in your community do you feel uniquely equipped to solve?

- **Set Goals with Intention:**

  - Break your dreams into actionable steps. For example, if your purpose is to combat food insecurity in your neighborhood, start by volunteering at a food pantry or learning about urban farming.

Step 3: Equip Yourself

A life of purpose requires tools to achieve your vision. This is where education—formal or informal—becomes critical.

- **Pursue Knowledge:** Whether it's going back to school, taking vocational courses, or watching free online tutorials, education is key to empowerment.

- **Develop Transferable Skills:** In many inner-city environments, entrepreneurship is a powerful vehicle for change. Skills like marketing, budgeting, or tech literacy can help you create opportunities where none exist.

Step 4: Stay Rooted

Living on purpose in the inner city requires perseverance. Challenges will come, but staying grounded in your values and vision will sustain you.

- **Lean on Faith and Spirituality:** For many in Black communities, faith is a foundation for resilience. Whether through church, meditation, or ancestral practices, connect with a source of spiritual strength.

- **Surround Yourself with Positivity:** Create a circle of accountability—friends, family, or mentors who encourage your growth.

- **Focus on Legacy:** Purpose isn't just about you; it's about the impact you leave behind. How will your life change the trajectory of your family or neighborhood?

The Role of Family

Family—especially a spouse and children—often holds up a mirror to who we are and who we want to become. Seeing your loved ones depend on you can awaken a sense of responsibility and drive to change.

- **A Partner's Support:** A loving, supportive spouse can encourage you to see your potential even when you can't. A partner might hold you accountable while also believing in your ability to grow. Has your wife ever challenged or inspired you in ways that sparked transformation?

- **Your Kids as Motivation:** Children remind us of the legacy we're building. Watching them grow—and imagining the life you want them to have—can inspire major change. Knowing that you're their example of strength and resilience makes every step toward growth worthwhile.

When life feels chaotic or dysfunctional, family can ground you. For many, they are the reason to keep fighting.

- **Unconditional Love**: Even when you fall short, the love of family reminds you that you're worthy of a better life.

- **Shared Dreams:** A strong family builds dreams together. You may have begun to think not only about your own goals, but also about what you and your wife wanted for your children—education, safety, stability, joy.

For many, having a family shifts the focus from self-centered concerns to building a future for others. Responsibility becomes a motivator for growth.

- **Breaking Generational Cycles:** You may have realized you wanted to be the one who breaks unhealthy patterns—of dysfunction, poverty, or limited opportunity—and give your children a different example to follow.

- **Accountability:** Being a husband and father can add clarity to your purpose. You're no longer living just for yourself; you're leading a household. That responsibility brings direction and urgency.

Legacy

You mentioned your wife and kids were central to your transformation. That ties directly into the idea of legacy. Legacy isn't just what you leave behind—it's what you live every day for your family to see.

- **Living by Example:** Every step you take—healing your past, starting a new job, learning to communicate better—teaches your children how to face life's challenges. They're watching and learning from you.

- **Creating Stability:** Your transformation likely brought your family greater emotional and financial stability. It's about giving your kids a foundation strong enough for them to dream bigger than you ever could.

- **Leaving a Mark:** When your children tell their own stories one day, your transformation will be part of their history. What legacy are you building for them right now?

Practical Steps: Building on Your Transformation

If your wife and kids were your inspiration, it's worth thinking about how you can continue growing for them—while also nurturing yourself.

1. **Strengthen Your Partnership:** Stay intentional about your marriage. Date nights, open communication, and shared goals keep your relationship strong, especially when life gets busy.

2. **Spend Quality Time with Your Kids:** Be present—help with homework, share stories, laugh together. Your time is the greatest gift you can give.

3. **Teach Them About Resilience:** Share age-appropriate parts of your journey. Let your kids see that you've overcome struggles, so they know growth is possible.

4. **Invest in Self-Care:** Remember, the stronger and healthier you are, the more you can pour into your family. Don't feel guilty about recharging—whether through hobbies, exercise, or quiet reflection.

Chapter 5: Conclusion

Building better communication skills is a cornerstone of personal growth and transformation—especially when your journey involves healing, building stronger relationships, and living a purposeful life. Communication is the bridge that connects your inner growth to the people and goals that shape your world. Strengthening it supports lasting change in every area of life—family, community, and personal transformation.

1. Communication Strengthens Relationships

Improving communication deepens your connections with the people who matter most—your spouse, your kids, your friends, and your community. Healthy relationships are built on trust, understanding, and respect, all of which depend on clear and compassionate communication.

- **With Your Spouse:**

Open and honest communication creates a safe space where both partners feel heard, supported, and valued. It minimizes misunderstandings and helps you work together as a team to overcome challenges.

- *Example:* Expressing appreciation for your wife's role in your transformation reinforces her importance in your journey and deepens emotional connection.

- *Skill to Practice:* Active listening—really hearing her concerns or ideas without interrupting or preparing your response—shows you value her voice.

- **With Your Kids:**

Good communication builds trust and teaches emotional intelligence. When you communicate calmly and openly, your children learn to process emotions and resolve conflicts in healthy ways.

- *Example:* When your kids see you discuss a problem instead of reacting with frustration, they learn self-control and empathy.

- *Skill to Practice:* Age-appropriate conversations—adjust your tone and words to meet your children where they are emotionally and mentally.

2. Communication Improves Emotional Awareness

Developing better communication isn't just about what you say—it's about how you understand and express your emotions. When you communicate your feelings, needs, and boundaries clearly, you reduce inner tension and create space for authentic connection.

- **Why This Supports Change:**

Many cycles of dysfunction—like anger, avoidance, or withdrawal—stem from unspoken emotions or feeling misunderstood. Clear expression breaks these patterns.

  - *Example:* Instead of bottling up stress about finances, you might say, "I've been feeling overwhelmed about money, and I'd like us to work on a plan together." This invites teamwork instead of conflict.

  - *Skill to Practice:* "I" statements—express your feelings without placing blame. Instead of "You don't help with anything," try "I feel overwhelmed when I have to handle everything on my own."

3. Communication Builds Trust and Accountability

Open and honest communication shows others that you're willing to take responsibility for your actions and follow through on your commitments. This is vital for both personal growth and relationship repair.

- **Why This Supports Change:**

Transformation often involves mending relationships strained by past behavior. Clear communication shows that you're serious about your growth and ready to show up differently.

- *Example:* Saying, "I recognize that my actions caused pain, and I'm committed to doing better," helps rebuild trust.

- *Skill to Practice:* Transparency—share your intentions and progress so others can see your consistent growth.

4. Communication Inspires and Motivates

When you're clear about your vision and purpose, communication allows you to inspire others and invite them to join your mission. Whether it's your family, friends, or community, your words can ignite positive change.

- **Why This Supports Change:**

Transformation is often a collective journey. Your loved ones may not understand your goals unless you communicate what drives you and how they can support you. Clear communication motivates others to align with your vision.

- *Example:* Sharing with your kids why you're working to break generational cycles—like improving financial literacy or emotional health—helps them feel part of something bigger.

- *Skill to Practice:* Storytelling—when you share your "why" in a personal, relatable way, it makes your journey inspiring and real.

5. Communication Empowers Your Purpose

Living with purpose means learning to advocate for yourself and others. Communication is the tool that helps you express your values, set boundaries, and take action toward your goals.

- Why This Supports Change:

Especially for those overcoming systemic or personal challenges, being able to clearly articulate your needs and vision is critical for progress.

  - *Example:* Use your communication skills to mentor young people, collaborate in your community, or speak publicly to inspire others.

  - *Skill to Practice:* Assertiveness—state your needs and boundaries clearly while respecting others.

Strategies for Building Better Communication Skills

Here are some practical ways to strengthen your communication and keep it aligned with your transformation:

1. Practice Active Listening:

Focus fully on the other person without interrupting or planning your response. Use clarifying phrases like:

- "What I'm hearing is…"

- "I understand how you feel because…"

2. Develop an Emotional Vocabulary:

Learn to name your feelings accurately—words like *frustrated, anxious, hopeful, grateful*—to express them clearly. Tools like an emotion wheel can help expand awareness.

3. Use Non-Verbal Cues:

Pay attention to tone, facial expressions, and body language. Stay calm and approachable—these cues often communicate more than words.

4. Seek Feedback:

Ask trusted people—your spouse, a friend, or a mentor—how you come across in conversations. They may notice things you don't, like interrupting or withdrawing.

5. Reflect and Adjust:

After a conversation, think about what went well and what could improve. If needed, circle back and say, "I've been reflecting on our talk and realize I could have said that differently."

Positive Reflections to Close Chapter 5

1. Celebrate How Far You've Come:

Reflect on where you started versus where you are now. Transformation is never easy, and the fact that you've made it this far speaks to your strength, determination, and resilience.

"The version of you reading this chapter is not the same as the one who started it. You've grown, you've healed, and you're proving that change is possible."

2. Recognize Your Impact:

Consider the ripple effect of your growth—on your spouse, your kids, your friends, and your community. Your effort is already creating a legacy of strength, love, and purpose.

You're not just changing your own story; you're inspiring others, whether you realize it or not.

3. Acknowledge Your Resilience:

Every challenge you've overcome has strengthened your foundation. Maybe you've broken old patterns, rebuilt relationships, or taken bold steps toward your goals.

"Resilience isn't about avoiding challenges—it's about rising each time you fall. And you've proven your ability to rise."

Continuing the Journey

As you close this chapter, build on your success and prepare for greater growth ahead.

1. Keep a Vision in Front of You

- **Reflect on Your "Why":** Revisit what drives you—your family, your purpose, your legacy. Write it somewhere visible as a daily reminder.

- **Set Clear Goals**: Break your next steps into milestones. For example:

  - Strengthen family bonds through weekly family time or date nights.

  - Continue personal growth by seeking mentorship, learning new skills, or taking classes.

  - Give back to your community through volunteering or mentoring.

2. Focus on Consistency

Progress isn't always about big leaps—it's about showing up every day. Whether it's working on communication, being present with family, or pursuing your career goals, consistency builds momentum.

3. Stay Grounded in Your "Why"

- Remember what started your transformation—your family, your vision, your faith.

- Strategy: Create a personal affirmation tied to your "why."

Example: *"I am breaking cycles, building love, and creating a legacy."*

- Action Tip: Reflect monthly on your progress and realign with your goals.

4. Embrace Continuous Growth

Transformation isn't a destination—it's an ongoing journey. Stay curious and keep learning.

- Strategy: Invest in personal development.

  - Read *The Four Agreements* by Don Miguel Ruiz for mindset growth.

  - Join community or mentorship programs to stay inspired.

- Action Tip: Dedicate 30 minutes a day to learning, journaling, or reflection.

5. Nurture Your Relationships

Strong family bonds are the heart of lasting transformation.

- Strategy: Schedule intentional family time and create shared traditions—weekly game nights, Sunday dinners, or an annual family vision meeting.

- Action Tip: Have regular emotional check-ins with your spouse and kids to share how everyone is feeling.

6. Give Back to Your Community

Your transformation carries wisdom that can empower others.

- Strategy: Mentor someone, share your story, or get involved in local initiatives.

- Action Tip: Take one tangible step—volunteer, donate time, or collaborate with a community program.

7. Focus on Legacy

Legacy isn't only what you leave behind—it's what you live every day.

- Strategy: Keep a *Legacy Journal* where you write down the values, lessons, and dreams you want to pass on.

- Action Tip: Write a letter to your children sharing what you've learned and the hopes you have for them.

8. Cultivate Gratitude and Positivity

Gratitude keeps you grounded and focused on what truly matters.

- Strategy: Begin or end each day by writing three things you're grateful for—even small ones like laughter with your kids or a productive day at work.

- Action Tip: Create a family gratitude practice—invite everyone to share one thing they're thankful for each day.

Final Reflection

Transformation is not a one-time event—it's a lifelong commitment to growth, love, and purpose. Communication is the thread that ties it all together—the way you connect your healing to your relationships, your purpose to your community, and your vision to the world.

You've already proven that change is possible. Now, keep building, keep loving, and keep speaking life—into yourself, your family, and your future.

www.ingramcontent.com/pod-product-compliance
Lightning Source LLC
Chambersburg PA
CBHW060809110426
42739CB00032BA/3158